Heal Yourself

V.P. ROSIE

Table of Contents

Introduction

"An arrow can only be shot by pulling it backward. So when life is dragging you back with difficulties, it means that it's going to launch you into something great. So just focus, and keep aiming."

— Unknown

Undoubtedly, life can be so difficult at times, and can even box you in, beat you down with no bars to hold for support. Well, no one ever said that life was going to be a smooth one in the first place, but a good number of us were not properly prepared for how difficult things could be in our lives. In fact, overcoming the toughest times of our lives can seem like a fairytale fantasy, especially when we go through repeated setbacks and failures.

But, how are we expected to deal with the numerous storms of life? What would happen if the burden of responsibility becomes too great for you to handle? How are you expected to go through the challenging times, especially when there is little or no support from friends, family and even neighbours?

Are you going through tough times right now in your life and family? Well, my heart goes out to you. Just remember that you're not alone; challenges are not meant for one person. Everyone of us will experience trying times at some point in life. I sincerely feel your pains and hurts because I've been there several times in my life.

But I have resolved that instead of just keeping my experience to myself and to my immediate family and friends, I can actually share my story and lessons learnt from my trying times. Hopefully, it will encourage someone out there to pull through the tough times right now. The reason why I named my book, "Heal Yourself," is because we all have what it takes to heal our hearts from the hurts of life.

I understand the pain, the heartache, loneliness, and the feeling of failure. I understand how it feels when the system you thought was put in place to protect you fails you and leaves you to your fate. But I won't in anyway insult you by claiming that I know precisely what you're passing through because that's the last thing you would want to hear when going through the seas of hopelessness.

My goal is to transfer to you the knowledge that I gathered from my experience, share how I survived, and possibly offer a sliver of hope to you along the way. I believe that in every trial of life, there are lessons to learn and benefits to get as well. So, I hope that this book, as well as my story, inspires you to go ahead and overcome incredible odds!

CHAPTER ONE

My Journey: Overcoming Tough Times in Life

"All of life is a test and we all have our challenges to meet."

— Marjory Sheba

Going through difficulties and surmounting adversities, especially during trying times is undoubtedly a monumental undertaking. It even gets worse when you add the regular stresses that we all face in our fast-paced world, which includes spouses, children, finances, and several others.

Also, not in any way ignoring the fact that we have to deal with the random crisis that life sometimes throws at us – which sometimes becomes too much to handle. But, from my experience as well as from research, it can be a bit easier to overcome challenging times by adhering to certain strategies.

This is especially true for strategies that have been working for several ages and still remain effective today. With the right strategies, the tough times might no longer appear tough anymore. But, make no mistake; this doesn't imply that all of life's difficulties will suddenly disappear – that's not possible.

You should realize the simplicity, beauty, and miracle of life – life is indeed beautiful. It's a gift that has been given to us by our Creator – whoever you believe that to be. Well, you can revert to the spiritual oneness that binds all humans which flows through all fabric of life if you don't believe in a higher power.

I have experienced my fair share of challenges, as you will see shortly from my story. I've experienced the pain and torment of failure, rejection, loneliness and abuse. I have come to realize that life is not all about sunshine and rainbows, but I'm certain that life is actually what you make of it – so, what do you want to make of life? Although my story is simple, I hope that someone will benefit from it and won't have to suffer the pains I passed through. I hope that it would help you find a way to survive the hard times you're facing as well. You don't have to lose hope on everything.

"That which does not kill us makes us stronger."

— Friedrich Nietzsche

My story started shortly after I was born. Well, I wasn't even given the slightest privilege to enjoy life before the challenges started. I was just nine months old when my father died and my journey started right after that loss. My father was already battling cancer when I was born, and he didn't live long enough to see my first birthday.

When he eventually died when I was just nine months old, it kind of devastated my mum. She found it hard to make peace with herself when it happened, and at the same time, she had to take care of my elder sister and me.

I was living with my mom and my sister; my mother was now working really hard since she had to raise us. It was also obvious that she needed help in raising her two children.

I remember one day when I came back from school; my sister was very tired of the stress our family was experiencing at that point and she kind of transferred her pain on me. She was obviously not ready for such responsibility, but things didn't turn out as she wanted. So, our mom had to take care of me and I believe that she did her best for us.

I understand that it wasn't easy, especially now that I have my own children. My sister often hit me anytime I make any mistake at home, even when I didn't do anything that could provoke her. It was as if I was the one that caused all the problems in our home, though things were difficult for everyone.

I was just two years old when my mother started dating another man. This was supposed to be a relief to my mother, to me and also to my sister, but that wasn't the case.

He used to drink a lot and was also abusive. My mum and stepfather were always fighting and I often wondered why they act that way. I guess it must have been because he was always drinking, but what made him drink so often is what I find difficult to understand, even today.

It was really a hard time for all of us. When he came into our lives, it was very frustrating because his didn't help our mom –actually, he made things even worse. But that's not the point; the point is that I had a really hard childhood when sometimes we didn't have what to eat and my mom had to sell her own milk when she was breastfeeding my younger sister.

It was the only way she could provide food for us. She was working really hard to keep us safe in this life and gave all she could give even when she was feeling lost. It was when I grew up, that I started to understand that my mom was struggling to provide food for us.

I promised myself that day that I will do everything I can, in one way or another, to help make her life easy. I tried to do my best; I started helping my mom at home. In fact, I went into the streets, picking bottles and selling them just to bring some money for my sisters and my mom so that she could buy some food for all of us.

When I started going to school, things were really difficult for me as well because I was always worried about what would happen each day. I was worried about my mom and if there would be food for all of us. I was worried whether it would be safe for me to go home and how safe my mom and sisters were. Constant stress had negative impact on my learning.

I was scared of all the shouting and fighting that was going on each day at home. But I always believed that when I grow up, it would be much easier and then I could help my mom more and more. One of the things I noticed when I started school was that other children were also struggling just like I did and I really wanted to help them. Although I tried to do my best in school and at home, it was still difficult for me in school because I was always missing my home works.

I just wanted to help my mom with house chores, and when I've finished helping, it was already late and I would be tired and sleepy. So, even when I knew I was intelligent, I was having a hard time in school. It was difficult for me to understand why some people find it hard to live peacefully; they are always angry and can hurt the feelings of other people.

The situation of things in my home, made me feel unsafe. I was also frustrated and in pain – not just physical pain but pain in my soul. I told my mom that I don't want to experience the fights and shouting and that I do not want to sleep alone or go somewhere. I was terrified of everything – even my shadow. One of the reasons why I found the fights and shouting to be unbearable was because I was beginning to have headaches every day.

Dealing with Health Issues

While growing up, I was always confronted with different issues, and one of them was my health. One day, I began to experience terrible pain in my head. It was just so strong that I could hardly look at the light, so I had to sit close to the wall, further from the windows, to avoid light.

In fact, my classmates had to bring me home since I was in severe pain and this got my mom scared because she thought she would lose me just like she lost my father. So she decided to take me to the doctors and even when the doctors failed to diagnose what was specifically wrong with me, they at least said they would do their best to help me.

But for the doctors, I was like a good target to carry out some experiments. They knew that my mom couldn't do anything; we did not have money for treatment; in fact, we barely had something to eat. So they told my mom that they would take good care of me and make me feel better and my mom believed them. She sent me to the hospital, but unfortunately, after the treatment, the pain didn't improve, rather, it worsened.

I could feel the pain in my head so strongly that I couldn't even see a light. Again, I was taken back to the hospital to see a doctor. I asked if maybe he could help to solve my problem and somehow take away my pains so that I can live a normal life again.

Well, the doctor said: "Yes, no problem. We can help you; just take these tablets, and you will be OK."I did it just because I believed that they were actually helping me heal the headaches. But after taking the tablets they gave me for one week, I ended up in the hospital again and this time with more pains. The doctors told us that it was normal and a part of the treatment, that everything would be OK.

The doctors even went ahead to call other hospitals to find out if they could help, but no one could explain what was happening to me. I was not able to eat and started losing weight.

Soon, I actually ended up in a coma – I didn't know how long I was in a coma, but it was a really long time. Days, weeks, months.One of the things I remember was that I heard my mom crying so badly. She was praying for me and asking God to save me and that he shouldn't take me like he took my father.

I heard her saying those words; however, I didn't know what happened after that. With the serious headaches, I remembered asking; "Please, let me stay so I can help my mom and be better. I have not finished yet, there is still a lot of work for me to do and I want to help."

Well, I can't explain what happened next; whether it was a miracle or not, I can't say for sure, but I just woke up from coma and saw my mom crying. It was just unbelievable and magical! The doctors around were amazed to see me wake up from coma. And after a while, I just asked my mom about what happened and why she was crying.

She just replied, "You see, the doctors told me that they can't do anything to help you and that I just have to say goodbye." They asked her to bring the priest and prepare because most of my internal organs were no longer functioning; I was almost dying, and there was no hope that I would wake up from coma.

It's really hard to tell specifically whether what happened to me wasa miracle or not, but I believe that yes, it was a miracle. That was how I got my life back, and since my recovery, I have been working really hard – even harder than I have ever worked before.

I started getting stronger and stronger, and as I continued on my journey, I was becoming more conscious of the fact that I'm not alone, especially after my recovery. Although I didn't know who is with me (maybe God, the Highest one), one thing is certain, He who is with me has always been protecting me and keeps me going even in my really hard times.

Back to School Again

After I spent several months in coma, the doctors said I wouldn't be able to go to school and learn like normal children because the development of my body has been arrested for such a long time and that was a miracle that I am alive.

The kind of food the doctors said I could only eat were things like baby's food or similar foods. So for a couple of years – about two years – I was staying at home and the teachers were coming to teach me. It was a really hard time. It was not just difficult for me but also for my mom, who was struggling financially to take good care of us.

This was one of the things that motivated me to push myself really hard to do my best and learn as much as I can. After two years, staying at home alone with my mum, I got really tired, so I asked my mom if

I could see a doctor once again to find out whether there is a small chance that I could go back to school because I really wanted to learn.

So we did that. I went to see a doctor with my mom to ask if I could go back to school. They were scared to allow me to go to school because it would put me at risk, and I may die in the process. We discussed all the available options and finally, they decided to allow me to go to school.

I must tell you that it was one of the best days of my life. I was so happy to go back to school, to be able to learn again as a normal person and feel again like everything is normal. I was so excited that I could barely wait for that day to come – it was a new beginning for me.

When I finally started school again, it was really difficult for me at first because I had already missed so much in the past two years, so I had to do everything I could to catch up with the rest of the class. But the children were not helping out at all; they were rude to me and made very hurtful remarks about me, "you're stupid," "go back home," "this school is not for you," and more hurtful words.

They looked at me as someone who is not normal, and they felt that I wasn't smart enough to be in school. The things they said were really hurting and affecting my feelings and everything else. I tried to ignore them and their abusive words and just focus on my studies.

Sometimes when I visited the toilet, they would wait for me there, spit on me and say very horrible things about me. I often cried whenever I was coming back from the school; I found it hard to believe that they could treat me so badly in school, despite the health issues I had faced. All I just wanted to do was to be strong and to help my mom, so one day I could make her life better.

Despite the abuse I was getting from the children in my school, I was still working hard. Finally, I was able to recover my missing points in school and I started believing that I could do it; that I could study just like the rest of my classmates. This was an amazing feeling for me and it began to increase my confidence that I could actually do more. At this point, I also discovered that I could not just go to school, but I could also go to college or university to learn more and help not just my mom but other people too.

I began to have a positive outlook on life and started thinking of where I could go to and what I would like to do. In my heart, I found out that I would love to be a lawyer; specifically, a social lawyer so I could help people.

This is also one profession that can enable me to even help my mum, make her life better and richer as well. So I thought about all these things and it really gladdened my heart. I finished school even though it was really hard and sometimes I would even feel as if it's nearly impossible.

One day, while at school, a woman approached me and asked me if I would like to be a model. I was at first amused when she said it, and I told her that I wasn't beautiful or even tall enough to be a model.

She insisted and even invited me to her studio. When I got home, I still found it hard to believe that she was serious, but the next day, she was right there in school waiting for me.

Again, she was asking if I would like come to her studio to see them. She really wanted to work with me and since I would lose absolutely nothing by going, I agreed and visited the studio. When I got there, she asked me to walk just like models do and I laughed because I didn't really know how models walk.

But I tried, and she said that it was natural and then she said, "Would you like to work with us?" I was so surprised and asked her to give me some time to think about it. I needed more time to process what was happening and they agreed to give me a whole day to consider it. Finally, I accepted the offer.

As soon as I got home, I told my mom about the offer and she was surprised as well. But when I asked her if I should go, she agreed and told me to go for it. So, for about two years, I worked as a model and I even made some money to help my mom to provide for the family.

I was just so happy and I continued to work very hard because I still wanted to go to college after I finish school. I understood that as a model, you could enjoy it while you're young, but as you grow older, you may not be able to do it again. Of course, my sisters were kind of jealous of that, which was breaking my heart, as I did it in order to make their lives better.

I have always believed that family is one of the best supports any individual can ever get while growing up. The family is meant to help and protect us against the external forces in our environment. I needed the support and encouragement of my mum and sisters, but unfortunately, I didn't get one. I still can't understand why my sisters hated me; I wanted them to love me, but the reality was entirely different.

This, however, didn't deter me from moving on with my life. I had always desired to go to college and study law (specifically social law). So, regardless of the lack of support from my sisters, I was still focused on achieving my goals. I was determined to go to college.

Finally, I applied to study in the Law College, though I wasn't sure if my application would be successful. Actually, I wasn't sure of what I would do next if I failed.

I really needed someone to talk to at this point, but my sisters, as usual, would simply abuse me and tell me that I wasn't strong or smart enough to be admitted into the college. I continued to wait, and that was actually a nightmare for me. But one day, I was helping my mum in the farm where we had a piggery and poultry like I always did.

Our life wasn't really an easy one – it was like every day, you would have to fight a battle. But on this particular day, my mum called me and asked me to come home and she told me that someone wanted to speak with me. I went home and answered the phone call. It was the College. They said that my application was successful and also invited me to study with them. Of course, I quickly agreed and told them I would be there.

I didn't have enough money for studies, but my mum told me that everything would be okay. She told me to go, and I went to college the next day. They asked me several questions, and I answered them. They asked me if I would like to study law and which type of law I was interested in.

I had just two choices; business law and social law. I had already made up my mind that I would love to study social law, so I told them. Interestingly, they said - congratulations, you are invited to study social law at our college.

It was another exciting thing that happened in my life. My heart was racing because of the joy and excitement of the news. I remember the day I started my studies as if it was today; it was in September. It was not easy when I started because my mum had to borrow money to help me with the studies. I told my sisters and friends that I was going to study social law.

In the words of my elder sister, *"I give you one year, and you will quit, or they would throw you out of school because you're not smart enough."* It was so painful for me to hear her make such statements because I really wanted her to be happy for me, and I was looking forward to making life much better for everyone of us, including her.

After a while, I pushed her comments behind me and promised myself to work really hard to ensure that I finish my program, if not for anything just to prove her wrong. I sometimes had to skip meals because I hadn't sufficient money, but I was able to finish my first year. Unfortunately, I broke down and was very sick for some time.

My doctor told me that I might not be able to finish the studies because I had to stay in the hospital and receive treatment. They said that my body wasn't strong enough and it was dying without sufficient food. My weight at the time was just 45 kg, but I refused to abandon my studies.

My major problem was irregular meals not just because of lack of money, but also because my studies often started in the morning and ended at about 8 pm every day. There was really no chance for me to work to earn some money and support my education. The second year was very hard for me, but I still finished while also helping my mum in her farm and restaurant business.

My elder sister was trying to sabotage my education and make my mum not to give me money for the college. I don't know if she did it intentionally, but I was more focused on how I can make things work out. I reasoned that if I can rent a room and take a roommate who could live with me, and help me pay my rent, I will be able to save some money and finish my last year in college. So I decided to find a roommate.

I found a student who was studying medicine and hoped to be a doctor one day. I felt that she would be a good girl because I always felt that people who study medicine need to study very hard to succeed.

But her case was entirely different; for instance, she drank and smoked a lot.

At that time, I had already made new friends who were all supportive and eager to help me. But, I never imagined what my decision to accommodate her would turn out to be. I guess my biggest mistake was asking her to be my roommate. Perhaps, if only I had never offered her the chance to be my roommate, life would have turned out differently for me. It could have saved me from the nightmare which I'm about to share with you shortly.

One thing is true; I somehow managed to accomplish my goal of studying social law at the college. I was so grateful for everything that I had so far accomplished even though it was really hard for me, especially when everyone around me was saying that I couldn't do it because I'm not strong enough. Most people said that I would never finish, especially my elder sister that never saw anything good in me.

I was constantly fighting all their negative comments and actions almost every day. Deep in my heart, I was always making strong affirmations. I would always tell myself: "I can do it,""yes I can do it, I can make this happen." I was taking steps every day towards the fulfilment of my dream.

Although they were small steps, but I was taking them, and I continued to tell myself that I can do it and I did! Well, I almost did, until one day – I was broken again. Actually, I was broken so badly that it took me more than five years to stand up and speak like I'm speaking now and that's why I want to help everyone reading my story, right now, and as many people as I can.

CHAPTER TWO

The Darkest Hour

It doesn't matter what is happening currently in your life. No matter how hard it may seem – even when it seems impossible – just understand that everything is possible if only you can believe it. If you genuinely want to have it, then it is possible.

I felt maybe lost, and it was starting to turn into a big mess in my life. I always knew what I had to do and where I had to be, but at that moment I wasn't sure if I could finish my studies because of money. And when I took my roommate who was paying the rent, she wasn't listening and I didn't really like her lifestyle – she was drinking and smoking a lot, and did whatever she wanted.

For me, that wasn't the best way to live, but I depended on the rent she was paying. I found a boyfriend while in college, but it was not without some difficulties because I needed to study and work hard. It was like everything was falling apart.

I recalled a day we decided to go out along with my roommate – this turned out not to be a good idea at all. At first, I didn't think of anything bad, and then we prepared to go.

But suddenly, I had this feeling that something really bad was going to happen and I told my friends about it. They didn't listen to me and finally convinced me to go. Things seemed to be cool until we were prepared to go home. I wasn't taking alcohol, just juice but my roommate was drinking so much and didn't seem ready to leave even when we were ready to go home.

My friends said that if I want to stay, I can stay back with her. I wondered how on earth, I would leave my roommate drunk outside, vulnerable, and lost. I just couldn't do it and leave her alone. I felt that the best option was to help her, so I decided to take her home. My friends left and asked me to be careful. So I stayed alone with her. This was actually the biggest mistake I ever made.

At this point, she was already drunk and her reasoning has been affected badly even as I tried to bring her home. She was with some guys who were giving her more alcohol and the more I tried to take her home, the more she wanted to stay there with them.

I guess I was quite naïve not to see the red flag in the situation, and this sometimes haunts me whenever I have flashbacks of what happened on that day. The men were actually preparing the ground to have their way, and I didn't understand. I wasn't the partying type or the clubbing type, so it was almost impossible for me to realize that they had malicious intentions.

Eventually, I managed to call a taxi to take her home, but the same guys giving her drinks were still with her. They asked us where we were going, and she said "home". They asked which way and I was again just so naive to tell them the direction we were going.

They said it was the same direction as theirs and they asked if we could go with them. Well, I couldn't turn down the request so they entered the taxi with us. My roommate wanted to eat some food and we stopped for her and they still stayed with us in the car.

When the taxi finally dropped us, I told her that I was going home whether she wants to come with me or not. When I finally got home, I felt a bit relieved, so I washed my face and got ready to sleep. I put on my pyjamas and suddenly heard a knock on the door, and when I opened, I saw that she was by the door. Unfortunately, when I opened the door, I saw the men that were with her too.

I told her that it was too late and that we needed to sleep, but no one was listening to me. They all just came in and started drinking alcohol again. At this point, I was so afraid, and even my dog was beginning to get nervous. I wasn't feeling safe at home anymore, and I wasn't sure of what would happen if I take my dog out.

My roommate was still very drunk, and I remember that she and another man took my dog and went out. But while I was about to go out, the second man locked the door and said that if I ever scream, that he would kill me. I attempted to unlock the door, and run away, but he grabbed me, pushed me really hard to my bed. He was lying on me and said that if I ever try that again, he would kill me. So I froze and couldn't even move anymore. I could only see what was happening to me – as if I was just standing and watching myself from above. Like I wasn't there anymore, in my body.

I was so scared, I was shocked and was unable to move. I just started begging him to stop, but he wasn't listening to me, and no one could help me because he had already locked the door. I wept bitterly while he raped me. As soon as he finished what he was doing, he dressed up and ran away. I was almost naked because my clothes were all over me and I was in a serious mess.

I cried uncontrollably, and when my roommate came back, I started screaming loudly at her. I started shouting at them all to leave my room, and I really didn't want to see anyone again. The other man went out and thought that I was crazy. At that moment, it was as if my world has ended; I was shattered; I felt like I was in a dream world, in between the earth and the other world.

My drunken roommate asked me what was happening, and I told her that I was just raped and that it was her fault because she brought them into my house. She asked if I should call the police, but at this point, I didn't even know what to do. All I just wanted to do was to wake up from the nightmare, but it never happened because it was reality.

She called the police, and when we got to the police station, I couldn't provide sufficient information about them because I saw them for the first time. The police said they would help me find the person that did it to me. When we came back to my room, I just couldn't stay in it again; I found it difficult to think properly and I was dying inside me. I later found a note with a card and a name and I was asked to call them.

At first, I was confused and I didn't know what it meant, but my roommate called to find out who was asking for me. Guess what? It was the same man that raped me and as soon as I realized that it was the man, he started threatening me that if I ever call the police, he will kill me.

Things were beginning to turn for the worse at this point. All I just wanted was to finish my studies, get a better job and help my mum and family. I guess that was not going to happen anymore considering the situation I have found myself in right now.

This changed everything for me; I had so many questions in my heart but no answers, and it was as if my world has come to an end. I went to the police with the card and note and told them that the man was threatening me. As soon as the police saw the card with the name of the man, they told me to just go home and forget about it. I was already in a bad shape at this point, but this made matters even worse.

Apart from the fact that I was raped, I was being threatened by the same man that raped me, and the police failed to apprehend the culprit and consequently, I was denied justice.

My mum called me to ask what was happening to me and it dawned on me that I hadn't even told her. I just broke down and started crying; I felt so guilty, like it was my fault. My mum was expecting much more from me, especially with her sacrifice and everything and at that point, I felt like I had just let her down. She began to ask what was happening to me and I just didn't know how to break the news to her.

I overhead my sister asking about what was happening to me and I felt like I wasn't there anymore. There was no way in this world that she wouldn't know. She was one person that I could trust at this point in life, so I told her.

My mum hired a lawyer to help me, but it didn't solve the problem because the man that raped me continued to threaten to kill me. I couldn't sleep anymore because I was always having nightmares. My nightmares were both as a result of the trauma of being sexually abused and the threats I received. My mum was so confused and didn't know what to do.

Finally, she decided to call the presenter of a TV program where they talk about the things that happen to others. They came to our home and filmed me and showed it on the TV. This was the final disaster and I even forgot to tell you that the man earlier called my mum and offered us money, provided that she withdraws the film from the TV.

My mum decided to go and see him and find out if he would tell the truth or confess. When she got there, she had a tape which recorded all the conversation and she also gave it to the people working on the TV show and they added it to the TV show. What happened thereafter was like a nightmare. It seemed to me that I wasn't his only victim.

After the TV show, three or more people also called to recognize him and they said he was the same man that raped them too. They also did the second part and it was then I discovered that there were other victims as well.

It was one of the most painful moments of my life and I was feeling lost, ashamed, and so guilty. I felt like I was doing something wrong and was constantly blaming myself all this time. If only I had recognised the red flag when they were giving my roommate more alcohol with the intention of making her drunk and affecting her reasoning...But how would I have known what they had in mind?

Deep down in my heart, I just felt that maybe I did something wrong. I shouldn't have waited for my roommate, who even cared less about my welfare at the time. Maybe if I had gone home with my friends, this would never have happened.

When you're a victim of rape or sexual abuse, you often experience guilt and shame, and I was not spared either. I had my fair share of guilt, dirty feeling and shame. It was really a difficult time in my life. I will be sharing some useful tips to help all victims of rape and sexual abuse in another chapter because I know what I passed through. But for now, I will talk about what happened next to me after the rape episode.

CHAPTER THREE

Out in the Streets – Lonely & Betrayed

The effect of the rape case was quite exhausting, and threats were flying all over the place. My mum actually helped me as much as she could, but one day, she was tired and my sister was exhausted as well because all the things that were happening threatened not just me but my entire family. The man even sent his men to my home to threaten me and my family for some time and even break into my mum's restaurant were my sister was working.

When I reflect on what happened, I feel that my mum must have run out of options and was beginning to get frustrated especially with the threats and the way things turned out – she wasn't making much progress with all her efforts and resources. It wasn't as if she had all the money in the world; we were just managing our lives with the little money she made.

Things began to change suddenly in my home. One day, while we were sitting in the living room, my sister's husband finally opened up and said that I was the problem and that I had to go away. I was shocked but tried to leave the living room because I didn't want to be involved in the conflict.

But he wasn't ready to step down even as he came into my room and continued to blame me for everything and said that I had to leave home for good. I just couldn't believe that he could be saying something like that.

He continued to scream and push me away, and I hadn't the strength to resist him, especially at this point that I was down. So I had to leave the house and couldn't stop myself from crying.

The pain was just unbearable and I had nowhere to go; I was on the streets and I knew I couldn't go back home again to face my mum, my sister and my sister's husband. What hurt me the most was that my mum watched as her son-in-law pushed me out into the streets with no one to run to.

I felt serious pain in my heart – the pain of betrayal, and at that point, I wished that I would go to sleep and never wake up again. Fortunately, one of my friends called me and took me in, but I didn't want to stay there for long.

I realized that I was just alone in this whole world and no one wanted me except my friends who wanted and supported me. I stayed with my best friend, and the next day, I appreciated him for accommodating me but that I couldn't stay with him. Obviously, I knew that my life was a big mess.

I have always experienced miracles before and this was the moment I needed one desperately just to survive. Someone sent my best friend and told me that she just had a feeling that something is wrong with me and wanted to know about it.

I cried so much and summoned the courage to disclose that I was on the street and had nowhere to go. She told me to come to her place and stay with her. I stayed with her for a couple of months. While staying with her, I cried most of the time.

I cried not really because I was raped and denied justice, but I found it very difficult to understand why my closest family turned their back against me when I needed them the most. I cried because I was hated so much by my own sister who was supposed to be my closest friend and confidant. I often wondered whether she was truly my sister, and I have not been able to understand the reason why she never liked anything about me. In fact, she even tried to find a way to take some money from him and make a deal with him.

At this point in my life, I realized that I was now all alone in this world. I thought of my late father and wondered why he would ever leave me alone to pass through such pains. I didn't want to finish my studies anymore because, at that point, I didn't see any need for that again. But my best friend encouraged me; she told me that I needed to be strong and should never allow anyone to break me down.

I still find it hard to explain how I ever finished my education and got my degree, but I know that the support of my teachers and my best friend played a major role. Although I finished college, I was still confused and didn't know what next to do. All the time I was staying with my friend, none of my family members called me to find out where I was and what was happening to me except my aunt.

She was the only one that called to find out if I needed help and she did help me while staying with my friend. I was able to survive, but I was no longer living; I was just a shadow of myself. I didn't even know how I could help myself and live with what has happened to me.

But after my degree, my mum called and she came to see me after all this time, she just called me as if nothing had happened in the first place. She didn't even mention the fact that I was chased out of home. So I called my grandma to ask if I could stay with her until I decide on what to do with my life and possibly get job.

My grandma at first was sceptical about helping me because my sister told her that if she helped me, they would be disappointed. But I still called grandma after my degree program and asked her if I can come because I was so lost and lonely. She said I should come and stay as long as I wanted. My grandma did her best to assist me, and the same goes for my aunt and her husband.

Again, just like nothing happened, my mum came to visit my grandma and started talking to me as if nothing happened before. She didn't even bother to know how on earth I managed to finish my social law degree program. She didn't bother to know how I fed myself and took care of all my needs till I graduated.

She was still my mum, so I responded to her, but I was still wondering if it was really her. I never imagined that I would ever survive the whole ordeal, but I managed to survive.

It was a time when I was really angry. I was blaming and found it hard to understand why my family abandoned me. During those moments of my life, I felt so lonely in this world – no family to lean on in trying times – I was feeling lost. But, I have to move on, so I have forgiven them. Although they were not there when I needed them the most, I forgave them and right now, I feel great.

I still help them whenever I can, and I often support them even if they failed to support me. What I just want is to be better every day no matter what I face and to be thankful, especially when I remember that it was strangers that helped me. Just as someone once said, *"If you want help, you need to help somebody who needs help as well."*

The Proposal

One of the things that I never imagined was having was a family of my own, a husband, and children. If I must ever live a normal life again, then I would need to see a psychologist. My husband, who was formerly my boyfriend, was very supportive during my trying times. Sometimes, I wonder why he had to stay with me despite my terrible shape.

I was merely existing, and who would like to live with someone like that? But he did, and when I look back, I realize that he was actually one person that was sent to assist me to pull through my mess. One day, I was shocked to hear him tell me that "You would need a good man who would help you."I was surprised to hear him say such a thing. So I remember when my grandma said something to me; it was like someone hit my head.

My grandma once told me that if you are in a terrible situation and find a man who loves you, stays with you, and helps you, then that is true love. It was like a dream; everything seemed to stand still at that point and I asked; why do I need someone like that? I still can't explain how I managed to stay with him and how he stayed with me, but here I was and he proposed tome!

I asked him why he still loved me and stayed with me even when I was broken. He told me that he loved me and that's what matters. He stayed with me even while I was in the hospital and while I was receiving the threat messages. I accepted his proposal and we got married and those who attended were the closest people to me; my grandma, my aunt and her family, my godmother who loves me like her own daughter.

She really helped me, especially when I didn't even know how to help myself. I also saw my younger sister who I thought hates me. But, I can never forget that it was because of my older sister that I had to leave my home. My marriage ceremony was very simple and there was no special dress. What was important was that we love each other and we were prepared to live together in health and sickness.

CHAPTER FOUR

Escape from My Country: A New Beginning

After our marriage, my husband took me home and changed my life completely. We stayed with his parents the first year because I still needed some medicine to survive. But after the first year, we decided that since I could not feel safe in my country anymore, we had to leave. I was always receiving threat messages that I would never come back if I go to some places. We didn't tell other people about our plan, except my aunt who lived in England.

We decided to move on as soon as possible, so I called my aunt and asked if we could come to England and stay for a while and find work and where we could live. She told us that she would think about it, but we couldn't wait for her response. We just made up our mind and sold all the things we had to raise enough money for the trip to start a new life – a new beginning.

As soon as we got the approval that we can come, we embarked on the journey. It was a long, tiring journey across Europe.

We stayed at my aunt's place for a couple of months. My husband and I started working really hard too; I was just like a robot, working hard to start a new life. One day, we discovered that we were going to have a baby. It was the day I started to have a good reason to live. I tried all I could to improve myself and be a better person – a good mother. But, my aunt told us that we couldn't stay anymore with her because there wasn't enough space for us and the baby. So we moved to a tiny studio flat.

This was actually the first time I started feeling happy, although we didn't have all the household items, like furniture and TV set, we were even sleeping on the floor. I still felt very happy. This was our own home, though rented. I realized that I had to change and stop having that feeling that I don't want to live. I asked my husband if he can find a way to help me become a better mum and person.

We started looking for a psychologist and at the same time, my husband needed to work while assisting me with the normal pregnancy sickness. He was working very hard to provide for us. I started to learn English language and began to push myself to be ready for the baby. I was assigned to a psychologist but my English was terrible – I found it difficult to even have simple conversations.

As I kept learning, things began to get better. However, I continued to have the nightmares and was always waking up at night, screaming and crying. I can only imagine what my husband was going through all these years; it was really a difficult experience for him.

I had these nightmares for a whole five years, and even after having my baby, it was very hard. While I was still pregnant and waiting for the doctor to see me in the hospital, I received a call from the police that they wanted to see my husband and me. I asked why, and they said that they wanted to talk about the man who was threatening me, the man who raped me. He told them that my husband was threatening him, which was not true.

I told them that wasn't possible because we're no longer living in Latvia, but in England and he was now living with me. They now told me that they would arrest him, and this became another nightmare for me. This was just too much for me to bear – waiting for my baby and having to deal with the pressure from Latvia. But thank God for people who helped us overcome the challenges.

I wondered if I could ever survive if they had taken my husband while I was still pregnant. Well, thank God because I'm still living with my husband in England and now we've continued to work harder, my English was getting better and I had regular appointments with the psychologist.

I felt that it was the time I studied again so I decided to study English because it would help my children and now I can say thank you to my husband and children who stayed with me in spite of the challenges. I wonder if I could ever survive the whole five years without their support. Even after five years, I still try to be a better person and I hope we could live a normal life after all that I've passed through.

After some years in college, I started speaking by myself and I still felt that learning English wasn't enough. So, I decided that as soon as I was strong enough, I would start working to help my husband to make things easier for him. I tried to do my best and I was beginning to heal myself again. All the things that happened changed me in several ways, either in a good way or a bad way, but they totally transformed me.

Presently, I find it hard to trust people and they need to prove that I can trust them again. I understand what it means to be stranded and lost with nowhere to go in life. That's why I try to help as many people as I can who may be going through hard times.

I'm grateful to my husband who has really been patient with me; in fact, I sometimes find it difficult to understand why he still stays with me despite all the things that I've passed through and put him through. Whenever I feel like letting him down, I encourage myself to put in more effort to make him proud. One of the things we decided to do to make things easy for us was for me to learn how to drive.

The reason is that he was always the one driving me to anywhere I wanted to go and this was difficult for him. Despite the challenges with my language, working at home and at the factory, taking care of our son, I was able to achieve it.

One day, we had a car accident. Although our son didn't sustain any injury, my husband and I sustained a few injuries and when the ambulance conveyed us to the hospital, we were checked for possible injuries. At first, they thought I was okay – and there was nothing wrong with me, but that wasn't the case. I was informed that my husband had some broken bones in his back and he hit his head somewhere.

I was scared that I may lose him, but thanks to the nurses and doctors, he is okay now – though he still experiences some pains in his back today. I just understand that my husband really loves us.

After the accident, he went back to work the next day because he needed to take care of us. It's a painful experience for me to think about the sacrifice he was making for us. I lost my job because of the injuries and this made my husband the only person working and fending for our family. I often wondered whether he was OK at work or not.

We were faced with another nightmare when we discovered that my husband had a cyst in his throat and would need an operation. I couldn't believe that this was happening to us again, but thank God he is fine now, I really appreciate the doctors for their efforts.

Shortly after that, doctors found out that I had health issues as well. They suggested, if we were planning to have another baby, it was the best time to have it, as pregnancy would possibly improve my condition. We went home and talked about it and finally decided to have another baby because I really wanted to have a baby girl.

I would really feel fulfilled. We tried to have a baby a couple of times and at some point, I thought that it wouldn't happen again, but we did it. I tried to be careful so I don't lose the baby, and consulted my doctor whenever we noticed anything. For instance, we went to see a doctor when we discovered that I was breathing too fast. We talked about how my baby and I would survive the entire process.

Losing My Grandma

While I was pregnant, someone called me from Latvia, and I can't really remember who exactly called to inform me that my grandmother was dying. This saddened me again and I wondered if I could ever live a normal life. I was also pregnant and thinking whether it would be possible for me to see my grandmother again for the last time.

We went to see my doctor to find out if it was safe for me to travel to Latvia. Unfortunately, the doctor refused to allow me to travel; he said it would put my life and the life of my baby at risk.

My heart was broken into a million pieces when it dawned on me that I would not see my grandma again because she has always supported and advised me when I needed it the most yet I couldn't even say goodbye.

Even though I tried to call her every single day and also called my friend who was a doctor, to help her, she couldn't make it. I cried for a long time and felt so much pain in my heart, even as I battled to protect my child and ensure that no harm comes to my baby. My husband as usual was very supportive as he encouraged me to move on with my life.

I was actually pregnant while going for my driving classes; in fact, my instructor once asked me, "When are you going to have your baby?" "Oh, my doctor said it could happen any minute," I replied.

"No no no, you better not have the baby now; just wait until you finish your test."

He was scared that it could happen during one of my driving lessons. But, thank God, I passed my test before my baby girl came.

Arrival of our Daughter

Two weeks after I passed the driving test, my water broke and it was at night. I had some complications and I almost died, but eventually, my daughter came into the world. I love my baby so much and she's quite different. I had enough time to take her into my arms and shortly after that; I started bleeding.

My blood was everywhere, and the doctor started panicking and asked my husband to take the baby because they needed to save me. When I look back at what happened that night, I actually doubted if the doctors would be able to save me. I was getting weaker and cold as I watched my husband carrying the baby.

Deep within me, I was crying and didn't want to leave my children and husband. What I passed through without a father was a nightmare for me and I don't want that for my children. It must be the higher power that intervened that night and they were able to stop the bleeding. We stayed in the hospital for a couple of days to be sure I wasn't bleeding again before they could discharge me.

I almost forgot to mention that I received a call from my older sister asking for my forgiveness and that she was sorry for all the things that were happening to me. Although I was weak at that point, I felt better after receiving the call. My husband called my mum and they came along with my son to the hospital to see me and our baby girl. Before this time, my son would always talk to my baby while she was in the womb.

When they came to the hospital, my son kissed his sister for the first time. It was a moment that made me feel better and have good reasons to live again.

Although we had just each other (my husband and I), I'm thankful for his patience and support. He was there with me. He did absolutely everything to help me stand up again and I did stand up with his help.

All that time, I survived with my husband by my side; I was not alone. He was helping me a lot. I was working hard while also trying to understand myself. Remember that the first time it was really difficult for me and I even thought I was not going to survive, but it came as a miracle.

I did everything that I could to stand firm and be a better wife, a better mom, a better daughter, and a better sister. Although it seemed like I can't help because I actually needed help myself, I did everything that I was empowered for – I managed (we managed) to help others who needed help.

For example, we took in a young couple, relatives of mine, who seemed lost and didn't know where to start life. We provided them with housing, and helped them to find a job. We were helping people who needed help even when my family and I also needed help too. I should mention here that I was quite grateful and so happy that I could help someone else.

It made me feel like I can be that person I once dreamed of – the one who can help other people even though it's just a little bit to make the world a better place for all of us. It's not just that I was getting help from strangers; some people helped in my healing process, like Mary and Pam, two wonderful women from an organisation that provides help to people in need. They were always calming me down and helping me and we often talked a lot about my struggles.

Pam always told me that the extent of my struggles doesn't matter; instead, I should always smile and remember, "The storms always go away and the sun will always come up and shine." I will forever remain grateful to all the people that helped me when things were difficult for me – thank you so much.

Heal Yourself

"I say find one true friend to help you get through tough times."

— **Kelly Osbourne**

I still don't know why my family abandoned me. Maybe the whole experience was too painful for them. There was a time when I had just a couple of months to live in my friend's home and no one was helping me. But I am thankful to my friend; she took me in her home and helped me. Yes, she helped me to finish my studies even when all members of my family turned their backs on me and refused to help me.

I am grateful to all for their support – my family, my husband, and my children. Now, I have two children who are amazing, and I love them so much. They give me all the love I need, and I feel blessed and thankful for everything. It does not matter how difficult the journey was for me; we worked hard to ensure that we have a better life.

Every step I took made me feel so happy because it was making a difference not just for me and my family but also for others in society just like I have always wanted. So I had to come up with a new way to help others as well as my family too. Even though I was feeling lost; I didn't know what to do, where to go and where I should start from, especially after I finished college, I still survived.

Having to survive days of sadness, loneliness, and frustration caused me to think of how I can make myself happy and impact other people's life positively with my story. I understand fully well that there are so many people who still need help – my parents, friends, and family. This is the real motivation for writing my story and this book to remind everyone experiencing difficult times, that they are not alone. I was once in their shoes and now things have turned for the better and they too can look forward to better days.

Undoubtedly, we all have some difficulties in our lives; everyone's got a different story. We all have our struggles even though most people pretend that everything is fine but I can see it in their eyes when something is wrong with them. I actually observed that some people feel ashamed to admit that they are struggling or that something has gone wrong. I want to use this book as a medium to tell you that you don't need to be ashamed; it doesn't matter what is happening to you, if you need help, just tell someone you can trust. Look for someone who is willing to help you and they will help you.

Just say what is on your mind and you will find people who are ready to help you to overcome all your difficulties. You're not alone; you need to shine and be better for everyone. Help each other and you will see that we can make this world better for everyone, including our children who are the biggest blessing that we can ever have.

Keep trying and if you have problems like anger or exhaustion, you can always contact me and I will share the experiences that I had while I was struggling. Don't be shy. If you feel you want to cry, you can cry because it will help in your healing process.

My message is – even with the hurtful experiences that we have, we all need to keep trying. We need to keep pushing further just like I did when faced with the challenges of life.

If you have problems, always remember that the storm will never last forever; the sun will spring forth and make all things better. We all have to find a way to heal ourselves and live a meaningful life. Never give up, move forward and continue to explore ways to make things work again.

Yes, all our experiences would be different, but one thing remains the same and that's the determination to keep moving in spite of the challenges you face. You can survive and live your life because life will always continue to move on – it never stops.

We all have to find a way to live a fulfilled life and enjoy the best of life. Yes, we can survive, we can find new ways to trust again, to love again and have a new life. Remember, crying does not make you a weak person; in fact, it is an integral part of your healing process. So don't be ashamed to cry, go ahead and let out the pains out of your heart.

You will certainly heal yourself of all the pains and hurts you have experienced before. Some amazing people are ready to help you, so go ahead and find them, and you should also be prepared to help others as long as you are in a position to do it.

Find the things that make you happy and do it; you may love reading, walking, sports, watching the movies, just find it and do it. I wish you the best in your life endeavours and I want to say thank you to all who are reading my book and I believe that it would add value to your life.

I'll share more about this in another chapter on how to deal with your hard times. Go ahead and do things that you love, visit places you love, meet new people and find new ways you can grow because if you are closed to people, you can never grow. You must have an open mind to new things. This is one of the best ways to move ahead and overcome your setbacks.

CHAPTER FIVE

Overcoming the Pain of Trauma

I have decided to dedicate one chapter to talk about sexual violence, especially when we consider the increasing rate of rape and sexual violence. I have discovered that one of the best ways to overcome challenges in life is to reach out to others in need, especially when you have what it takes to help them. So, this explains why I decided to share some information and knowledge that I have gained from experience and research regarding the issue of rape.

In the United States, for instance, many women are now coming out to talk about how they were sexually molested in the past. The Centre for Disease Control and Prevention (CDC) revealed that almost one in five women in the US are sexually assaulted or raped at some point in their lives usually by a person they trust or know.

This figure is even higher in some African, Asian and Middle Eastern countries. Sexual assault isn't limited to women only – a good number of men and boys are also victims of rape and sexual trauma every year. Regardless of gender or age, one thing is certain – the impact of sexual violence involves more than mere physical injuries.

From my experience, I can tell you that the trauma of being raped or sexually assaulted can be shattering. It can leave the victim ashamed, scared, and alone. In fact, just like my case where I was being threatened by the rapist; sexual assault can cause victims to be plagued by nightmares, flashbacks of the incident and unpleasant memories.

The world no longer feels like a safe place, and it becomes very hard to trust others including yourself as well. You now begin to question your self-worth, your sanity and also your judgment. Just like I did, you may start blaming yourself for the things that happened, or you may feel that you're "dirty" or "a damaged good."

It causes relationships to feel dangerous and intimacy may even be impossible. That's not all; some rape survivors also end up struggling with PTSD, depression and anxiety. I must state here that what you're experiencing after being raped or sexually assaulted is a normal reaction to trauma. I experienced it then and I understand how it feels.

Your feelings of shame, self-blame, defectiveness, and helplessness are all symptoms and not your reality. Regardless of how difficult it may seem, you can overcome them and live a very normal and exciting life. I actually got to the point where life was no longer worth living; in addition to my trauma, I was rejected by my family and I was lost, wandering the street with no idea of what to do next.

So, in response to the pains and experiences I have gone through as a rape victim, I have assembled some tips and techniques that I applied which will help you come to terms with what happened and also enable you to regain your sense of trust and safety while learning to heal and move on with your life.

But first, a lot of myths have been circulating about rape and sexual assault and I think it's a great idea to try and dispel the toxic and victim-blaming myths regarding sexual violence. This will undoubtedly be a great way to kick-start your healing process.

Common Myths & Facts about Rape & Sexual Assault

Myth #1. If you failed to fight back, then you must not have thought it was that bad.

Fact: Understand that during a sexual assault, it is extremely common to freeze. This implies that your brain, as well as your entire body, can simply shut down in shock, which will make it very hard for you to move, speak, or even think.

Myth #2. You can easily identify a rapist by his looks or actions.

Fact: One of the things I suffered was being blamed for the whole thing that happened. It's often one of the things that further increase the pain and traumatisation of rape victims. It has been proven that there is absolutely no sure-fire way to recognise a rapist. Many rapists appear friendly, completely normal, non-threatening and charming. So, identifying them by their actions is not always possible in all cases.

Myth #3. Date rape is usually a misunderstanding.

Fact: In most cases, date rapists defend themselves by claiming that an assault was because of miscommunication or too much alcohol. However, research has suggested that most date rapists are repeat offenders. They simply target vulnerable people and ply them with alcohol just to rape them.

Myth #4. Rape victims often "ask for it" based on the way they dress or act.

Fact: You should understand that rape is just a crime of opportunity. I was only helping my drunken roommate when I met the man that raped me for the first time. He took advantage of my roommate that was already drunk to enter my room and ended up raping me.

That was just the perfect opportunity for him to strike and not because of what I was wearing or how I acted. In fact, studies have revealed that rapists select their victims based on their vulnerability and not because of how flirtatious they are or how sexy they appear.

I had no one to come to my defence at home; he already locked the door and my roommate left with the other man. This made me very vulnerable and I ended up being a victim.

Myth #5. If you've had sex with the person before, then it's not rape.

Fact: A person is not given a perpetual right to your body simply because you've previously consented to sex with the person. If your boyfriend, lover, or spouse forces sex against your will, then it's nothing but rape.

Steps to Help you Recover from Rape or Sexual Trauma

Now that we've dispelled some of the toxic and victim-blaming myths about sexual violence, let's focus now on steps you need to take to start your healing process and recover.

1. *Talk about what happened to you*

Admitting that you were raped or sexually assaulted can often be an extremely difficult thing to do – there is usually a stigma associated with it. I remember when my mum called me after I was raped, I found it extremely hard to open up and tell her what happened. I was even feeling ashamed of myself.

The reason for this is that rape can make you feel dirty and weak. Also, you may doubt how others will feel or react when you tell them that you were sexually assaulted; will they look at you differently or judge you? At this time, it's often easier to downplay what happened to you or even keep it a secret altogether.

However, you can only end up reinforcing your victimhood when you remain silent and deny yourself help. The best option is to reach out to someone you can trust. In my case, I reached out to the only person in my life that I trust and that was my mother.

One mistake rape victims often make is to think that if they fail to talk about how they were raped, then it didn't really happen. Unfortunately, avoiding the truth is definitely not the best way to heal. In fact, hiding can only add to the feelings of shame.

Although opening up might appear to be a scary thing, it will set you free. But, while reaching out to someone, you must be selective of who you tell – especially the first time. I would suggest that your best bet is someone that is empathetic, supportive and calm. In case you don't have someone you trust enough to talk to, then you can talk to a therapist.

2. Challenge your sense of Isolation and Helplessness

One of the negative effects of trauma is that it renders you powerless and vulnerable. This implies that it's crucial to remind yourself constantly that you have great strengths and coping skills that can help you overcome difficult times. You can reclaim your sense of power by helping others – so volunteer your time or reach out to a friend that's in need or donate to your favourite charity.

Consider joining a support group meant for rape or sexual abuse survivors. One of the benefits of belonging to a support group is that it will help you to feel less isolated and lonely. Also, most support groups can provide you with invaluable information on how to cope with the symptoms and focus on recovery. You can search for an online support group if you fail to find one in your area.

3. Coping with the Feelings of Guilt & Shame

While it's not too difficult to understand intellectually that you're not to blame for the rape or sexual attack, you may find yourself struggling with a sense of guilt or shame. Such feelings may manifest shortly after the rape incidence or several years later.

However, it would be easier for you to fully accept that you're not responsible as you acknowledge the truth of what happened. You didn't bring the assault on yourself, so there is really nothing to be ashamed of here. In most cases, the feelings of guilt and shame often emanate from misconceptions earlier mentioned:

✓ You failed to stop the assault from happening: Remember, after the incidence, it's usually easy to second guess what you did or didn't do. Well, you may fail to remember that while in the heat of an assault, your body and brain are in shock. So, it becomes very difficult for you to think clearly. For some victims of rape, they disclosed that they feel "frozen" at that moment. You don't have to judge yourself for this natural reaction to trauma. Bear in mind that you did the best you could under extreme situations. *If it was possible for you to stop the assault, you could have done it.*

✓ Trusting someone you shouldn't have: This is perhaps one of the most difficult things to deal with after being raped or sexually assaulted by a person you know. It is clearly the violation of trust, but questioning yourself and wondering whether you missed several warning signs is a natural reaction. But don't blame yourself – the person to blame here is your attacker. Don't beat yourself up for believing that your attacker was a decent person; instead, your attacker should be the one to feel guilty and ashamed.

4. *Dealing with Flashbacks & Upsetting Memories*

Generally, when our body experiences something stressful, it temporarily enters the "fight-or-flight" mode. As soon as the perceived threat has passed, our body will calm down. Unfortunately, traumatic experiences like sexual assault and rape can make your nervous system to remain stuck in a state of high alert.

This causes you to be hypersensitive even to the smallest stimuli. This is very common among many rape survivors. Some of the things commonly experienced, especially within the first few months after being raped include nightmares, flashbacks and intrusive memories.

If your nervous system is still "stuck" in the long-term, you may end up developing post-traumatic stress disorder (PTSD) and this may last much longer. Here are some tips to help lower your flashbacks and upsetting memories:

✓ **Anticipate and be ready for triggers:** Generally, some of the most common triggers include places that are associated with the rape and in my case, I had two places; the place where we went to hang out and my room. Other triggers include certain smells, sights and sounds and anniversary dates. Once you have discovered the possible triggers that may lead to an upsetting reaction, you will be able to properly understand what is happening and find ways to calm down.

✓ **Focus on your body's danger signals:** Our body and emotions offer us clues anytime we begin to feel stressed and unsafe. Some of these clues may include holding your breath, shortness of breath, feeling tense, dizziness, hot flashes, nausea, and racing thoughts.

✓ **Take actions immediately to self-soothe:** As soon as you've identified any of the symptoms earlier mentioned, it's crucial that you quickly take actions to calm yourself down before it spirals out of control. Slowing down your breathing is one of the most effective and quickest ways to calm anxiety and panic. You can soothe panic by practicing this simple breathing exercise.

> ✓ Stand or sit comfortably making sure that your back is straight. Place one of your hands on your chest while having the other one on your stomach.

> ✓ Then slowly breathe in through your nose while counting to four. You will notice that the hand on your

stomach is rising as you do it while the one on your chest has to move slightly.

✓ Hold onto your breath and count to seven.

✓ Exhale via your mouth while counting to eight and make sure that you push as much air as possible from your body while contracting your abdominal muscles. As you do this, the hand you placed on your stomach should move in while the one on your chest will move slightly.

✓ Again, inhale and repeat the entire cycle until you now feel relaxed.

Strategies for Dealing with flashbacks

It's not always easy to prevent flashbacks; however, if you discover that you're losing touch with the present or you're feeling like the rape incidence is taking place all over again, then you can take these steps.

✓ First, accept and reassure yourself that this is just a flashback, and it's not happening in real-time. Remind yourself that the traumatic experience is over and you have survived. You can make use of this script anytime you're in this situation: *"I'm feeling overwhelmed, panicked and frightened right now just because I recalled the rape/sexual assault, but right now, all I can see around me is that assault isn't happening and I'm no longer in any danger".*

✓ Endeavour to ground yourself in the present: By leveraging grounding techniques, you will be able to redirect your attention away from the flashbacks and focus on your present environment and situation. For instance, you can touch your arms or describe your real environment and the things you see around you – you can even name the place where you're currently staying, three things you see as you look around and the current date.

5. *Go ahead and Reconnect your body and Feelings*

Don't forget that your nervous system may be in a hypersensitive state because of the rape or assault. So, you may begin to numb yourself or avoid all associations with the trauma. However, it's possible to selectively numb your feelings. For example, whenever you shut down the unpleasant sensations, you also shut down your self-awareness and capacity for joy.

This makes you disconnected physically and emotionally – you only exist but not fully living. Some of the common signs that you're numbing and avoiding in unhelpful ways include:

✓ Feeling separate from your surrounding and body - You feel as if you're just watching yourself or the situation you find yourself instead of participating in it.

✓ Feeling physically shut down - You no longer feel bodily sensations the way you used to; in fact, you may find it difficult differentiating between pain and pleasure.

✓ You may find it difficult to remember things or even to concentrate.

✓ Escaping through daydreams, fantasies, video games, excessive TV, etc.

✓ Making use of stimulants, physical pain, and risky activities just to feel alive and also counteract the empty feeling inside of you.

✓ Feeling detached from the people in your life, various activities you used to enjoy and the world.

✓ Compulsively making use of drugs or alcohol.

If you must recover after being raped, then you have to reconnect to your body and feelings. I remember going through similar conditions, though I didn't resort to the use of drugs to help numb my feelings. However, you will remember clearly when I mentioned that I was just existing and didn't see the reason to live.

My desire to begin to live was revived when my husband proposed to me in spite of my terrible situation. It was at that point that I asked him why he would still want to marry me despite all that I have been through. It even got better when I realised that I was pregnant. I understand that it's a frightening experience to get back in touch with your body as well as your feelings after experiencing sexual trauma.

In many ways, rape causes your body to become your enemy – something that has been violated, contaminated and need to be hated or ignored. Also, it's often scary to experience the intense feelings that are associated with the assault. However, even though the process of reconnecting may feel threatening, it's not dangerous.

Understand that even though feelings are powerful, they are not your reality – they are not capable of driving you insane. But you may be exposed to real danger to your physical and mental health when you start avoiding them. As soon as you're back in touch with your body and feelings, you will begin to feel more confident, powerful, and safe. To achieve this, consider the techniques below:

- ✓ **Embrace Mindfulness meditation:** There is no particular location you need to practice mindfulness meditation– you can practice it anywhere – while eating or walking. Just focus on what you're feeling in the present movement and this includes other bodily sensations and emotions. Your aim is to observe without judgment.

- ✓ **Rhythmic movement:** Rhythm helps us to relax and also regain a deep sense of control over our bodies. It can actually be very healing. Things that combine rhythm and movement will do you good like marching, drumming and dancing. In fact, it's also possible to incorporate it into your running and walking routine and concentrate on the back and forth movements of your legs and arms.

- ✓ **Massage:** You may also feel uncomfortable with human touch after being raped, however, being raped does not erode the fact that touching and being touched are a crucial way we can give and receive comfort and affection. One of the ways to begin and reopen yourself to human contact is through massage therapy.

6. *Stay Connected*

Since it's often common to feel isolated and disconnected from other people after a sexual assault, you may be pushed to withdraw from social activities and even from your loved ones. However, it's crucial to stay connected to life as well as other people who care about you. Sometimes, I wonder what my life would be like if I had not met my husband. He was very patient with me and he understood what I was going through. He was not judgmental.

Your recovery will greatly be enhanced by the support you get from other people. But don't forget that support does not always imply that you have to always dwell on what happened before. You must go ahead and participate in social activities even when you don't feel like it. Reconnect with your old friends and also make new ones.

7. *Help Someone else Recover from Sexual Trauma or Rape*

Now that I have provided useful information to help anyone who has been raped or sexually assaulted before to recover, you also should do the same. Do you have any loved one that has been raped? Let the person know that you still love them and try as much as you can to reassure them that it wasn't their fault. Don't be in a hurry to hear their story and pains, give them some time to open up at their pace.

This is because sexual assault victims often find it very hard to share their experiences. You can also encourage them to seek professional help. I was unable to deal with the nightmares that I was having, and after suffering for a long time, my husband and I decided that I should see a health professional. I can tell you that my life has since become better with fewer nightmares.

CHAPTER SIX

The Forgotten Truths about Hard Times that Will Help You Overcome

"Success is not final, failure is not fatal: it is the courage to continue that counts."

— Winston Churchill

Just like my experience, the most loving, wisest and well-rounded people you've ever come across are most likely people who have known defeat, heartbreak, misery, and people who have lost someone or something they loved dearly. But they were able to find their way out of the depths of their despair.

Since they have experienced several ups and downs in the course of their lives, they have gained appreciation and sensitivity as well as an understanding of life which fills them with understanding, deep loving wisdom, and compassion. Note that such people weren't born like this; instead, they developed such traits slowly over time.

If you take a look at my story, you will discover some of these traits and I developed them as I continued to overcome incredible odds. I discovered that people are going through difficult times just like me and while I needed help, I also needed to help others.

While growing up with my mum and sister, there were days we could hardly afford food and I have through such experiences learnt to be grateful for the little things that I have gained. In this section, we shall be looking at some powerful but easily forgotten truths about hard times, which will help you choose wisely and increase in strength while going through the toughest times of your life.

Our approach to hard times is a vital aspect of our survival, so you need to understand the lessons we can get from difficult times. Information is key and although you may forget some of the points here when going through challenges, chances are that some may stick to your memory and help you overcome.

I remember one of the encouragements of Pam and it helped strengthen me in trying times. She told me that the extent of my struggles doesn't matter; instead, I should always smile and remember, "The storms always go away, and the sun will always come up and shine." What are some of the lessons we can learn from difficult times?

"Anything that annoys you is for teaching you patience. Anyone who abandons you is for teaching you how to stand up on your own two feet.

Anything that angers you is for teaching you forgiveness and compassion. Anything that has power over you is for teaching you how to take your power back. Anything you hate is for teaching you unconditional love.

Anything you fear is for teaching you courage to overcome your fear. Anything you can't control is for teaching you how to let go and trust the Universe"

— Jackson Kiddard

Pain is Part of Life & Love: It Aids in our Growth

This shouldn't frighten you in any way, though it may actually sound scary. In fact, many of us are afraid of our truth, ourselves and also our feelings. Most times, we express how great the concepts of love and life are, but the truth is that we end up hiding from both on a daily basis.

I have discovered that sometimes, life and love can hurt and we get disturbed by the feelings this brings to us. Right from the time we were born, we were taught that pain is evil and harmful, but how can we ever deal with real life and true love when we're scared to feel what we truly feel.

Just as we need to feel alive and loved, we also need to feel pain because pain is meant to wake us up. One of the best ways to know how strong you are is when the only choice you have is being strong. How do you handle the things that fail to go your way? I have had several moments when things didn't go the way I wanted.

For instance, I never wanted to be raped, but I was forcefully raped. Things didn't go my way, but I had to move on with my life. In fact, things got so bad that the law enforcement in my country that was supposed to protect me failed to do so and even further exposed me to more risk. When I was raped, the man threatened to kill me if I ever report the case to the police and once I did, then my life was in danger. What truly matters is how you handle the things that fail to go your way.

Pain is a feeling and your feelings are part of you; they are part of your reality. You will only allow the lies of insecurity to destroy your reality by feeling ashamed of your feelings and concealing them. You need to stand up for your right to feel pain – you have the right to endure it.

Don't be scared of the scars - own it. This is how you can deal with the realities of life and love and even grow into the truest, wisest and strongest version of yourself. I refused to allow the insecurities I faced in my country to hinder me. I moved out of my country and was able to find a place where I could live without the fears of being abused again. Pain is part of life and love, stop running from it, face it and grow stronger.

It's Crucial to Keep things in Perspective

During your moments of trial, it's often easy for all your problems to be blown out of portion and make you lose perspective of your reality. Sometimes, we end up allowing our challenges to become too big for us that we become fearful and paralyzed from either making the right decisions or moving forward to carry out the changes that will solve the problem and ease our pains.

Be careful not to let fear to stop you from making the changes you need to make. Yes, you should acknowledge your fear, but deal with it as well. Let your focus be on the things you can do and also focus on engaging in small daily tasks and small steps.

Thinking of the future is great, but at the moment, focus on the small things that matter. Small actions will definitely lead to solving the big problem in the future while eliminating the fear and intimidation caused by big problems.

Failure is a Crucial Aspect of Success

"Develop success from failures. Discouragement and failure are two of the surest stepping stones to success."

— Dale Carnegie

It's never possible to achieve great things without obstacles and failures. No one has been able to explain the reason for this and neither do I, but that's just the way life is. One of the reasons why most people fail to make efforts in life is because they are afraid of failing or making mistakes.

In their hearts, they keep thinking about what would happen if things didn't work out and then become scared to encounter setbacks and adversities. Unfortunately, all great successes happen to be on the other side of failures and obstacles. This implies that you have to first overcome the failures before you can start enjoying the successes.

Well, I would advise that you avoid going after shortcuts because there are none. You should never be scared of making a mistake – it's OK to screw up sometimes and if you want to screw up, screw up big. You can never be killed by tough times, setbacks, mistakes, adversities and obstacles. I would never have believed that I could survive all the things I passed through in the middle of the crisis, but I survived.

If I can still overcome the nightmares of being raped, abandoned to my fate by the law enforcement that was meant to protect me and now being threatened by the same person that raped me, then you can live and become successful despite the trials and setbacks on your path. All you need right now is to persist and hold on tight.

The culture we live in often conditions us to embrace the easy fix, so many of us believe in the magic bullet that is capable of bringing us success. For instance, people love the idea of taking weight loss pills instead of something harder like exercise; we prefer the easy route over the more difficult route that's also more fulfilling.

When facing hard times, instead of confronting our reality, we numb our feelings with alcohol and drugs. We become scared of adversity instead of embracing it. This also applies to those of us with big goals; we usually get so obsessed with accomplishing those goals that every small sign of challenges and setbacks will turn into a burden.

All the things that fail to go exactly as we wanted it is a problem and turns into a blow to our ego. A good number of people are unable to stand failure and adversity, so when they fail once or twice, that's it. Take a look at my story; I was in my final year studying social law when I was raped and rejected by my family.

In fact, my elder sister, as I earlier mentioned never wished me well in my studies. She had been hoping and telling me that I won't last more than one year in College. So, I guess when I was raped, it served as the right time to ensure that her prediction came to pass.

Fortunately, I managed to hang on to my dreams and with the help of friends, I finished my studies. You don't have to give up on your dreams and goals simply because you feel that you're not good enough, tough enough, or smart enough.

I have discovered that it's a natural tendency for humans to want the easy life – win a lottery, then go on vacation at the beach daily until you die. I can't say that having such kind of life is bad, but if you're interested in seeing how great you can be, then you can't avoid adversity.

If being successful in life is easy, everyone would have been successful; if being fit and having that perfect shape is easy, then there would not be fat and obese people around us. What makes success great in the first place is because it is hard!

Come to think of it, if it were easy to be a billionaire, then every one of us would be enjoying life right now on our yacht. But what makes being a billionaire great or what makes having that perfect body shape great is because it's hard. That's precisely what separates the people who are committed to their success in life from those who are not.

If you are genuinely interested in achieving great things in life, then you must also be prepared to face the things that great people face – obstacles. You must be prepared to confront your challenges and overcome them. After having several nights of nightmares and living in fear of being attacked, I had to face my fears and deal with it.

I had to meet with a psychologist who helped me overcome the nightmares; it could have made my life more miserable, but I refused to allow it. Don't be the type that works toward achieving your goals when everything is going the right way for you and quickly gives up when adversity hits you.

Refuse to make excuses or look for reasons why success isn't for you or blame other people or bad luck for the poor results you're getting in life. If you truly desire to succeed in life, then you must accept the fact that every victory requires some adversity.

Bad things don't last forever

Remember, the sun doesn't shine all the time and neither does the rainfall all through the year. This also applies to difficulties and obstacles that you are facing right now. It may be hard for you to believe that what you're facing now is only temporary, especially with the pain it's causing you. Well, life is created in a way that trials and setbacks are temporary – they will someday fade away.

The duration of the trials is something we may not be able to predict, but it still has an expiry date. The hard times you are facing right now are not meant to cause you to fail; rather, they are there to ensure that you pass so that you can enjoy the great times that are ahead of you.

We may experience the rain, the sun, the snow and even have thunderstorms, but they are never going to last forever, they will certainly stop at some point. Things will come and go, but one thing that remains the same is change. So, have the courage to face the tough times you're going through right now.

I remember when I was on the streets with nowhere to go, abandoned by my family; I felt that this was finally the end and there was really nothing else to live for. But, when I look back today at what happened to me, I now realize that it has helped to strengthen my resolve to do well in life in spite of what comes my way. You can draw strength and inspiration from my story.

Challenges make us stronger

Take some time to consider this; have you ever grown from solving easy tasks? When was the last time you said "Wow, I've become a better person this month" because everything was going so smoothly without a single challenge coming your way? Chances are that there aren't such cases.

The reason is that every one of us grows in storm and not when things are calm. It's almost impossible to develop new skills when you're very comfortable. Although comfort zones are always the nicest places to be just for a while, you must avoid staying there for too long because you might end up not growing as you would have wanted.

Just as you go to the gym to improve your muscles, that's how you also improve your mindset. We need some kind of resistance to develop muscles and have six-pack for the men or lovely curves for the ladies. You may not make good progress with your weight loss and muscles if you continue to lift the same easy weights for a very long time.

But when you provide your muscles with variation and challenges, then they will adapt and grow. This is exactly how our mind is programmed to work. You have to push through some resistance if it must grow.

When next you encounter a challenge or fail to accomplish your goal, rather than give up, see it as an opportunity to increase your mental strength and also increase your chances of succeeding subsequently. You will find some tips to help you overcome your challenges and achieve your goals in the next chapter.

CHAPTER SEVEN

How to Get Through Hard Times

"Your mess is your message! Your resilience comes from not giving up on yourself; figuring it out is the most beautiful adventure that you'll ever have."

— Misty Totzke

As earlier promised, I will share with you some useful tips to help you overcome hard times and emerge a stronger and better person. I have experienced several challenges of life; I have been in coma and almost died. Doctors at some point almost gave up on me, they told my mum that I might not survive.

I have also experienced financial challenges while growing up. There were times we could barely eat and had to engage in several jobs just to put food on the table. I have been raped before and denied justice – I'm well qualified to talk about hardship and its impact on our lives. I can confidently tell you that when you strive to overcome all the difficult experiences facing you, you can heal yourself!

If you're currently going through similar difficulties that I experienced or have gone through it before – loss of a job, a house, a romantic relationship, or a friendship – you can heal. Regardless of the kind of stressor in your life, the tips below can help you pull through and emerge stronger and better.

#1. Acknowledge Your Feelings

The starting point to your healing is to feel your feelings. Although avoiding all your negative emotions may feel like a stopgap measure that's very effective, it's merely aiding in postponing, escalating and even exacerbating the flood of negative emotions in the future. You don't have to be ashamed of crying when you are down because ignoring your emotions is just like "attempting to run away from something placed on your shoulder."

The best way to free yourself is to face your emotions. Although your emotions might be overwhelming, most people end up being stuck simply because they are ignoring their emotions. Rather, they think about it, replay events, and allow in it. But they often fail to allow themselves to feel the pain, sadness, loss as well as anger within them. You can take advantage of the TEARS method. It stands for:

✓ Talking

✓ Exercising

✓ Artistic expression

✓ Recording of experiences

✓ Sobbing

This method can help you cope with your emotions, especially when grieving. They provide you with what to do anytime you're feeling overwhelmed by the stresses of life.

#2. Be Inspired by Others who Overcame Similar Challenges

Although people can easily relate tothe experiences of popular individuals that failed and later became successful in life, we're not always familiar with their journeys. However, it's their journeys that actually resonate with most people since they understand what they passed through before their success story. From my experience in life, I have realized that nothing in life that's worthwhile will ever come easily.

The process of achieving success in life can be a bit less arduous if only we can reach out and find inspiration in other people around us or those who have achieved similar goals that we want to achieve in life. This is also an excellent way to deal with tough times and overcome the storms of life. Every one of us needs inspiration; we need hope, and there are many books on this topic which will help you greatly.

Those who have overcome incredible odds in life and went on to be successful understand that life is just a series of peaks and valleys. There are times we may find ourselves up and the next time we're down. Although we need the support of each other at all times because no one is an island, it is during our down moments that we need more support and guidance.

Go ahead and leverage the stories of successful people who have passed through similar challenges you're going through and became successful. You can listen to TED Talks or search YouTube for inspirational stories. One of the books that people going through tough times should read are biographies.

All biographies contain the stories of ordinary people who were not restrained by their challenges and unfavourable circumstances. It contains stories of men and women who pushed through and became successful in spite of the impossible situations they found themselves. When you read biographies, it helps empower you – if they could do it, then I can! You become renewed and consoled that you're not just the only one going through such trials.

#3. Talk about your Feelings and Experience

Our problem often grows and mutate into horrible worries and anxiety the moment we bottle up our challenging situations. But when we talk about our challenges, we will be able to understand our fears and also receive valuable feedback from other people who might have passed through similar kinds of distress and provide you with the right perspective to solving the problem.

#4. Find Opportunities to Help

Remember, while sharing my story, I mentioned that although I needed help, I tried as much as I could to help others in need. One of the best ways to make it through challenging times in life is to make a positive impact on the life of others. I know you may be wondering how you can impact other people without having enough money.

You don't need all the money in the world to help others, you can invest your skills, time and other non-monetary resources. So, ask yourself right now, what can I do to help someone else today? This will shift your focus tremendously and as you begin to contribute to others around you, you're actually sending a strong signal to your subconscious mind.

By giving your skills, time and other resources to help others, you're letting your mind know that you have more than enough. Although you may not think of it consciously, this is precisely the kind of signal that is transmitted. Now the moment that thought permeates your mind, it will help provide you with a deep sense of gratitude.

Apart from realizing that other people around you might be in a far worse situation than yourself, you are definitely going to feel good about your actions. I have come to realize from several years I have been passing through challenges that life is all about contribution. Although humans might physically govern themselves based on the selfish-survival principle, that's not a true reflection of how many people around the world live their lives.

Many successful people give to others; they donate their skills, knowledge, expertise, time, etc. to assist others that are unable to help themselves. I can tell you that there isn't a better feeling than this. So, go ahead and think about this; search yourself and identify the little things you can do for others. Pick up a sheet of paper right now and ask yourself, "What exactly can I do for others today?" "How can I assist others that are down today?"

Remember, it's not all about money; you have other things that can make a tremendous change in other people's lives. In my opinion, time is one of the things you can offer – it's more valuable than any amount of money you can make because it can never be regained once lost.

#5. Engage in What Makes you Happy

One of the ways to get through your hard times is to engage in things that make you happy. So, the first thing you need to do is to ask yourself this: what makes me happy? As usual, pick up a piece of paper and write down all the activities you know will make you happy right now. There is no need to wait until later; you can write down as many as ten things that are capable of filling you with joy and elation. It may be driving to a far place in your country, reading a book, spending time with your children, chatting with friends, hiking, camping; just write them down.

The next thing you need to do is engage in one of the things that makes you happy each day. You can schedule time for each of the activities just like you schedule time for a meeting. Spend at least 30 minutes each day doing it. I know that this won't help to solve all your immediate problems, it can offer you momentary relief, especially during your toughest times in life.

#6. Make Self-care a Habit

One of the things you need to overcome adversity is self-care. In fact, you can never be of any help to others around you if you are incapacitated. Although you may have time for your usual healthy habits, you also need to create time to take good care of yourself. So, if you're unable to go to the gym, you can walk for 10-15 minutes to help relieve physical tension that you may be having. You can also spend some time meditating and rest sufficiently to help reboot your mind and body.

#7. Learn to Practice Acceptance

You need to understand that there are things we can control while others are not within our control as well. Your duty is to identify the things you can't control and let go of them. Get a sheet of paper and write down the things you cannot control right now in your life. Then go ahead and stop worrying about them!

#8. Ask For Help

It's easy for you to assume that you're capable of handling your challenges alone on your own. In fact, many people also expect others to manage their problems alone. It's crucial that we relinquish control and request for help and also accept it gracefully.

While asking for help, you need to be direct and make it clear to others around you that you need help. Clearly state the kind of help you need like compassion, support, etc. Also, don't forget to mention the things you don't need, like criticism, and judgment since they might slow down your healing process.

Although I was deprived of the support and love from my family, getting support from your loved ones and family can indeed quicken your healing process while strengthening the relationships too.

Friends and family members who can listen, be there for each other, share experience, talk about things and feel together openly, can help hurting people heal faster and also protect and strengthen the relationships in stressful times. You can get support from co-workers, family, therapist, doctors, friends, support group and also your higher power.

#9. Spend Less Time with Toxic People

I still wonder what would have happened if I didn't wait to take my roommate home when she was drunk. The company you keep matters a lot; spend time with negative people and over time, they begin to influence your life.

As much as possible, you need to spend less time (or no time at all) with toxic people. Most people regarded as toxic are not reliable or supportive. They don't actually have your best interest at heart.

Some of them might be demanding, judgmental and critical and they won't have the time to listen to you. When you hang around with such people, you will feel drained and depleted – a worse situation. What you need is to stay with people who can help your healing process.

#10. We all Heal Differently

No one has the right to monitor you in life; we all feel differently and also heal differently. Understand that difficult times can feel incredibly exhausting and overwhelming. However, you can soften the blow in several ways. Don't forget that you can seek professional help if you're currently in crises and you need someone you can talk to – someone you trust. Don't forget, *"The best time to fix the roof is when the sun is shining."*

This implies that the best investment of our time and effort is to deal with relational issues, abuse issues, childhood issues, or anything we may be dealing with when we're in moments of relative calm. Understand that hardships are just opportunities for growth and learning and you can only get stronger and better.

Final Thoughts

It has been a long journey as I shared my story, my journey so far as well as my healing process. In the heat of your challenges, one thing you must always remember is that it can never last forever. The challenges are only for a moment and will soon give way if only you can persist long enough.

There are many people who couldn't persist long enough and ended up losing out in life. You hardly hear such stories because we see them in society – those who have lost hope and are no longer interested in making efforts to become better.

Your goals in life as you heal from the hurts and abuse you've experienced so far is to remain focused and never turn back on your dreams. Your healing process may not be instant – just be patient as you continue to improve each day until you can finally stand on your feet again.

I hope that my book will help you; that it will help you find inspiration and hope. It doesn't matter the extent of obstacles you may be facing; you can always get better. All that you need to shine is inside of you, so go ahead and shine.

Sources

Chernoff, M. (n.d). 10 Forgotten Truths to Help You Get Through
   Hard Times. Retrieved on August 6, 2019 from
   http://www.marcandangel.com/2014/06/01/10-forgotten-
   truths-to-help-you-get-through-hard-times/

Gamliel, A. (n.d). Overcoming the Unthinkable. Retrieved on
   August 6, 2019, from
   https://www.chabad.org/theJewishWoman/article_cdo/aid/10
   14243/jewish/Overcoming-the-Unthinkable.htm

Robinson, T. (2019). 10 Simple Things You Can Do To Get
   Through Hard Times. Retrieved on August 6, 2019 from
   https://www.lifehack.org/articles/communication/10-simple-
   things-you-can-get-through-difficult-times.html

Smith, M. A, & Segal, J. (2019). Recovering from Rape and Sexual
   Trauma. Retrieved on August 5, 2019 from
   https://www.helpguide.org/articles/ptsd-trauma/recovering-
   from-rape-and-sexual-trauma.htm

Tartakovsky, M. (2018). Therapists Spill: 14 Ways to Get Through
   Tough Times. Psych Central. Retrieved on August 4, 2019,
   from https://psychcentral.com/lib/therapists-spill-14-ways-to-
   get-through-tough-times/

Wanderlust Worker. (n.d). How to Get Through The Tough Times
   In Life. Retrieved on August 6, 2019 from
   https://www.wanderlustworker.com/how-to-get-through-the-
   tough-times-in-life/

Xuan, S. (2011). The Beauty in Challenge – the more you overcome it the stronger you will become. Retrieved on August 5, 2019 from https://www.pickthebrain.com/blog/the-beauty-in-challenge-%E2%80%93-the-more-you-overcome-it-the-stronger-you-will-become/

-

Printed in Great Britain
by Amazon

34238451R00055